Kid's Library of Space Exploration

ISS: The International Space Station

Kid's Library of Space Exploration

Kid's Library of Space Exploration

ISS: The International Space Station

Kim Etingoff

Kid's Library of Space Exploration
ISS: The International Space Station

Village Earth Press
Vestal, New York 13850
www.villageearthpress.com

First Printing
9 8 7 6 5 4 3 2 1

Series ISBN: 978-1-62524-012-5
ISBN: 978-1-62524-013-2
ebook ISBN: 978-1-62524-036-1

Library of Congress Control Number: 2014931521

Author: Etingoff, Kim.

Contents

ONE

Early History

People have dreamed about living in space for a long time. In the 1950s, we came one step closer to that dream when we launched the first human being into space. Soon we were landing people on the moon. We were even thinking about going to Mars.

Then, living in space became real. With the invention of space stations, people can now live in space for days, weeks, and even more than a year at a time!

The biggest space station is called the International Space Station (ISS). Fifteen countries help run the station. Astronauts from many countries make trips up to it.

The ISS is relatively new. But the idea for space stations is a lot older. In fact, that idea for existed even before people sent anything up into space.

From Idea to Life

The first time anyone came up with the idea of a space station was in the nineteenth century. An American writer named Edward Everett Hale wrote a short story about a brick moon built by people.

The brick moon was sent into space with humans aboard. They survived and lived on the fake moon. As far as we know, this is the first time someone thought of having people live on something made by humans in space.

That was in 1869. Fast-forward about a hundred years, and people were actually creating the *technology* needed to let people live in space.

The first space station was launched by the Soviet Union in 1971. It was called *Salyut 1*. A few years before, the United States and the Soviet Union had been in a "space race." Each country was *competing* to see who could be the best in space.

The Soviets had sent up the first satellite into space. They also sent up the first person. But then the United States landed the first person on the moon. The United States had won the race to the moon.

After that, the Soviet Union decided to focus on a different goal. They had lost the race to the moon. But they could still do a lot in space. They turned to the idea of a space station.

They built *Salyut 1*. They launched it and it stayed up in space for 175 days. It circled the Earth almost 3,000 times. Compared to today's space stations, it was fairly small. But it was a big first step.

Salyut 1 was launched into space without anyone on board. Just a few days after it entered space, though, the Soviets sent up a spacecraft to bring three men up to the space station. Unfortunately, the door didn't work when they got there! The *cosmonauts* couldn't get in.

A few weeks later, three more cosmonauts went up to the space station. This time they got in. The three men stayed on board for about three weeks. That was the longest anyone had ever been in space.

Sadly, all three cosmonauts died on the way home. A panel

Technology is something humans invent or use to make a task easier.

Competing means trying to beat each other in a contest.

on their spacecraft came open during re-entry into the Earth's atmosphere. The inside of a spacecraft has just the right *air pressure* for humans. When the panel came open, the pressure changed, and the people on board died. After that, anyone going into space started wearing spacesuits during lift-off and re-entry.

Salyut 1 had a short life. The Soviets crashed the space station into the ocean (on purpose). Then they sent up some more short-lived space stations.

Meanwhile, in the United States, everyone was paying more attention to going to the moon. But then NASA (the National Aeronautics and Space Administration) decided to work on a space station for the United States. NASA had gotten people to the moon and back. Now it was time for the next project.

NASA built the *Skylab* space station. Several crews went up to the station. They did scientific experiments. They also showed the world what it was like to live in space. Up until then, no one really knew for sure that people could live in space for weeks, months, or years at a time. Astronauts on space stations like *Skylab* helped scientists figure out how to help people live in space.

Skylab had several complicated parts. The crew lived and did experiments in the orbiting workshop. The *airlock module* let the astronauts safely go outside. The station also had a dock that let more than one spacecraft enter at the same time. *Skylab* had telescopes too, so people

Cosmonauts are members of the Russian space program. It's the word Russia uses instead of "astronauts."

Air pressure is the force of the air around you pressing on you. There is no air pressure in space.

An *airlock module* is the part of a space station that astronauts enter and exit through.

Why "Space Station"?

Scientist Hermann Oberth first came up with the term "space station." He thought a lot about space travel. One of his ideas was a wheel-shaped spacecraft that would circle the Earth. People could live on it and prepare for longer journeys into space, like to the moon and Mars. He called his idea a space station. In fact, we still think of space stations in the same way today.

Part of Skylab's *purpose was to see the effects of living in space for long periods of time.*

could look deeper into space and see new things.

Skylab flew in space until 1979. Eventually NASA *abandoned* it. *Skylab* fell to Earth and burned up over the ocean. Some parts even fell on western Australia, but no one was hurt.

When something is **abandoned**, you give up on it and leave it alone.

A "Permanent" Space Station

The *Salyut* space stations were sort of like practice. The Soviets were getting ready to launch a longer-lasting space station called *Mir*. *Mir* means "peace" in Russian. *Mir* was a lot bigger and heavier than the *Salyut* space stations. Although *Mir* wasn't meant to last forever, it was designed to stay in space longer than any previous space stations had.

Mir also lasted a lot longer. It stayed in space for fifteen years. In all, it circled the Earth 86,000 times, almost always with people on board. One person, Valeri Polyakov, even spent more than a year living on *Mir*!

The new, more permanent space station had lots of parts and equipment. The crew had living quarters where they could be comfortable for months at a time. There were also several different modules, used for different kinds of experiments. The Spektr module, for example, was used to do experiments with the Earth's atmosphere. And *Mir*'s dock had space for several spacecraft.

Mir stayed in orbit until 2001. Lots of scientific experiments were done on the

A Rocky Start to *Skylab*

Not everything went exactly according to plan when *Skylab* was launched. About a minute after lift-off, a meteoroid shield on *Skylab* opened up and then broke off. After that, a solar panel fell off. The space station was in trouble before it even got into space. The station didn't have much power, and it was hot because it wasn't shielded from the sun. Luckily, the first crew to work on *Skylab* fixed it. They got another solar panel working, and also cooled the space station down. The repair was the first time people had fixed a space station while it was in orbit.

The Space Shuttle Atlantis *docks with the* Mir *space station. NASA's space shuttles were often used to transport astronauts to and from space stations.*

space station. Cosmonauts did biological experiments. They did physics experiments. They looked into space and did astronomy experiments. Space stations gave humans an entirely new lab where they could figure out how the universe works.

The ISS Idea

By the end of the twentieth century, the world was ready for a new space station. The *Mir* space station was getting old. It would cost a lot to repair it. The United States didn't even have a station in space.

Lots of countries wanted to create the next space station. The United States was trying to develop a new space station called *Freedom*, but it was never built. *Freedom* would have cost too much money. People were less interested in space exploration at the time, and the government didn't want to give NASA so much money.

In Europe, the European Space Agency (like NASA in the United States) was working on the *Columbus* project. *Columbus* would be part of a space station. The European countries would attach it to Freedom. Japan was developing a similar part, which was also going to be attached to *Freedom*.

In Russia, scientists were trying to build a new space station called *Mir-2*. That station was also never built.

Scientists from the United States and Russia met in 1993. They talked about combining their projects. In the end, they came up with a new plan. Several countries would help build the International Space Station. The United States would be a big part of it. So would Russia. Japan and Europe would also have parts in the International Space Station. Every country would have to pay only a part of the cost, which made people happy.

The International Space Station would be like a city in space. The

American and Russian crews worked together on the Mir *space station—and continue to do so today on ISS.*

main purpose was to see if humans could live for long periods in space. Someone would be living on the ISS almost the whole time it was in orbit. Some astronauts might even live there for over a year.

Eventually, the ISS would be preparing people for even longer periods in space. Once scientists learned what living on the ISS was like, they might be able to figure out how to send astronauts to Mars or beyond!

Find Out Even More

Reading books is a great way to learn. But a book like the one you're reading now can only hold so much information. The book's author had to pick what to put into the book and what to leave out. Even though reading a book like this is a great way to learn about the things that you want to know more about, there's a lot more to learn.

One book can never hold all the information about a single subject. To get a full view of a subject, it's best to look for more than one source. One of the best places to start looking for information is your school library or public library. Try looking for the books listed below in the library's card catalog. Searching the electronic card catalog by title, author, or subject are all good ways of finding books you're looking for.

Holden, Henry M. *The Coolest Job in the Universe: Working Aboard the International Space Station*. Berkley Heights, N.J.: Enslow Publishing Inc., 2012.

Nipaul, Devi. *The International Space Station: An Orbiting Laboratory*. New York: Children's Press, 2004.

Scott, Carole. *Space Exploration (DK Eyewitness Books)*. New York: DK Publishing, 2009.

If you can't find these books, try looking for books with the same subject. Even if you can't find these books, the library will probably have other books on the International Space Station or space exploration. Ask the librarian for help if you're having trouble finding the kind of books you're looking for.

Take a look at each book you find. Read the table of contents near the front of the book. Check out any chapters that seem interesting to you. Leaf through some of the book's pages. Once you've taken a look at the book, ask yourself a few questions:

1. Is there any information in the other book that wasn't included in this one? What did you learn from that book that you didn't learn from this one?
2. How much of the book did you understand? Did you feel like you understood each word, or were there some words that you didn't understand? Not every book is the same, and not every reader is the same, either. Sometimes, you have to find a book that suits your reading level. That doesn't mean you can't read a book that challenges you. But finding the right book for you is a big part of becoming a better reader and learning more from the books you read. Remember that many books have a glossary to help you understand important words. Check the table of contents or the back of the book for a glossary.
3. How do the pictures in the book help you understand the book's ideas? Do you think they added to your understanding of what the book was about?
4. How is the information in the book organized? Can you look up information quickly using the index in the book? Does the table of contents help you find the subjects that you want to read about most? How is each chapter broken up?

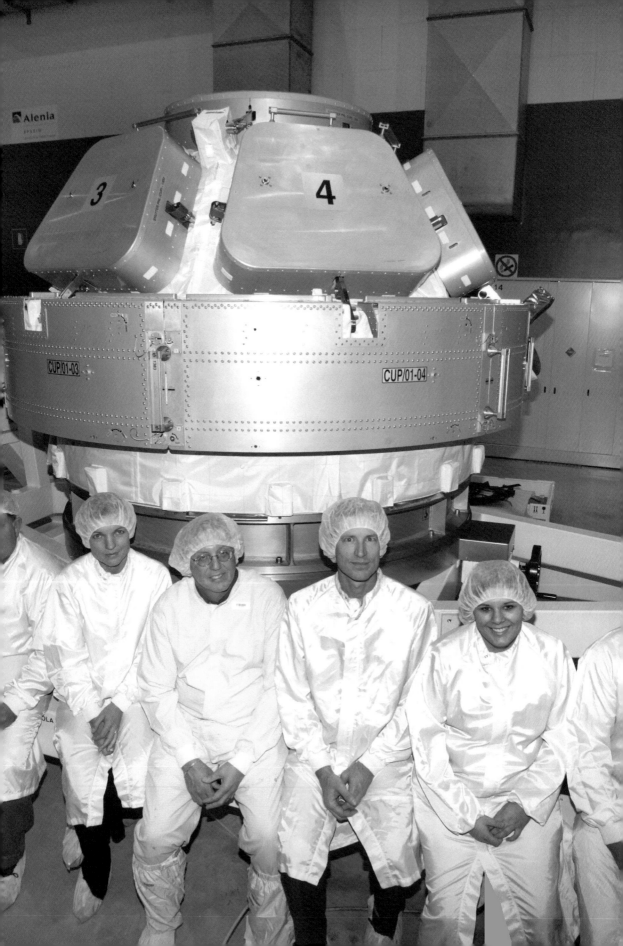

TWO

Building the ISS

Building the International Space Station was going to take a lot of teamwork from people around the globe. Scientists from fifteen countries had to work together to get the ISS into orbit.

People were up to the challenge. In the end, the world would have a brand-new space station circling the Earth, ready to give us lots of new scientific knowledge.

Working Together

Several different space programs had to work together. NASA is from the United States. Russia has its Federal Space Agency, which is also called Roscosmos. The European Space Agency, the Canadian Space Agency, and the Japan Aerospace Exploration Agency were also working on the project. Each administration had its own way of doing things. But they have all figured out how to work together to make the ISS.

Although the United States couldn't build the American Freedom *space station that they had hoped for, many of the design elements from the* Freedom *project were used in the International Space Station.*

Astronauts from different countries also live together on the ISS. Americans, Russians, Canadians, and astronauts from many more countries have all flown into space and lived together on the ISS. It's called the *International* Space Station for a reason!

Putting It All Together

The ISS was too big to put together on Earth and launch into space. People would have to build it piece by piece and put it all together in space.

The largest pieces of the ISS are called modules. Each module does something different. Some have laboratories. Some have space for the crew to live in. Some have lots of computer equipment.

Other parts on the outside of the station keep it stable and safe. Several solar panels give it power. And several docking ports allow spacecraft to attach to the station to let travelers in and out.

The first module launched into space was built by Russia in 1998. The Zarya module was launched into space on a rocket. It has storage space and fuel tanks. A month later, the United States launched the Unity module. The ISS was growing.

Building the whole ISS took fifty space missions. Finally, in 2008, the ISS was done. However, astronauts had already been living on it since 2000. Just two years after people started building the ISS, it was ready for use. Two cosmonauts from Russia boarded, and they called the ISS home for five months. Since then, humans have always lived on the ISS.

Some of the other modules include the Destiny laboratory. Astronauts use it to test how materials and technology work in space. The

Countries' Contributions

Here's a list of some of what each country added to the International Space Station project when it first started:

- United States: several space station modules, a laboratory, solar panels, life support, navigation system, communications system
- Russia: research modules, solar panels, spacecraft to bring astronauts to and from ISS
- Europe: laboratory, logistics transport vehicles
- Japan: laboratory, logistics transport vehicles
- Brazil: equipment
- Canada: robotic arm

The Unity module was the section of the ISS that connected pieces that the United States and Russia built seperately.

Zvezda module is where the crew lives. And the Columbus lab has places to do experiments in physics and biology.

These modules are just the beginning. Here are some of the major parts of the ISS:

- Canadian Mobile Serving System: made up of a 55-foot robotic arm used for maintenance and putting things together.
- Russian Service Module/U.S. Habitation Module, where the crew lives: has bathrooms and places to eat and sleep.
- Crew Return Vehicles: extra spacecraft the crew can use in case they have to return to Earth in an emergency.
- Automated Transfer Vehicle: brings extra supplies and fuel to the ISS.
- Japanese Experimental Module: a laboratory for space experiments. Part of it is actually outside the ISS, so astronauts can do experiments in exposed space.

The Space Shuttle Program

One of the main goals of NASA's space shuttle program was to bring people and equipment to the International Space Station. Several shuttles connected Earth and the ISS before the shuttle program was retired in 2011. Now, astronauts travel to the space station on Russian space shuttles called Soyuz shuttles.

The space station's measurements are impressive. It weighs almost a million pounds. It is 167 feet long. Its eight solar arrays are 240 feet long. In all, the ISS takes up the space of a football field!

So far, the ISS has proved that people can safely and even somewhat comfortably spend a long time in space. Lots of experiments have been done, and we've learned a lot about living in space.

Find Out Even More

Reading a few books on the International Space Station is a great way to learn more about it. When you read a book, the author has already gathered information and put it together for you. She's put it together in a way that will be easy to understand. A lot of work goes into finding just the right facts to put into a book like this. But no book can hold all of the facts about a single subject.

Searching for information online is a good way to learn even more about the International Space Station or anything else that you find interesting. If you want to learn more about a subject, using a search engine is a great way to get started online. Search engines like Google, Yahoo!, or Bing help to find the sites you want to visit on almost any subject.

There is no limit to the amount of information you can find online, so it's helpful to have search engines to help find just what you're looking for using a few important keywords. Keywords are words that are important to the subject you're searching for. Here are a few keywords you might want to search for after reading this book:

International Space Station
NASA
Freedom
Mir
Skylab
astronauts

Soyuz
Salyut
space tourism
Mars
space shuttle

If you search for any of these keywords using a search engine like Google, you'll get millions of search results. That means millions of websites to learn from about almost any topic you can think of.

THREE

Life on the Station

Before space stations, people had spent only a few days in space at a time. Getting to the moon and back didn't actually take very long. We knew that it was possible for people to survive in space. But could they survive for longer periods of time? What would living in space for six months or more be like?

The ISS was designed to answer those questions. Scientists and astronauts have figured out how to live in space, at least for a few months.

Today, several astronauts—usually seven—live on board the ISS. In the past, there have been as few as two while the ISS was being built. But someone has been living on the ISS ever since 2000. Each crew lives on board for about six months.

Living in space takes some getting used to. Eating, sleeping, going to the bathroom—all those things are a lot harder when you're floating around in space! Fortunately, we've come up with plenty of ways people can survive comfortably aboard the ISS.

Russia's Soyuz spacecraft, seen here, is still used today to bring astronauts to and from the ISS.

Getting There

Astronauts first have to get to the ISS before they can start living on board. In the past, many astronauts got there on American space shuttles.

NASA built and used five space shuttles—*Challenger*, *Columbia*, *Endeavour*, *Discovery*, and *Atlantis*. The shuttles brought people back and forth from the space station.

Then, in 2003, *Columbia* broke apart when it was re-entering the Earth's atmosphere. All seven astronauts on board died. The space shuttle program stopped for a little while.

Eventually, the United States government and NASA decided to end the shuttle program entirely. They would send up a few more crews. Then they would retire the three shuttles that were left.

Now NASA had to figure out how astronauts were going to get to the ISS. They didn't want to stop sending people. NASA decided to send American astronauts on Russian spacecraft called *Soyuz*. They could basically buy the astronauts tickets.

Longest Space Flight Record

The person who has lived in space the longest is Valeri Polyakov, of Russia. He spent 437 days in space on *Mir*. Russian Mikhail Tyurin and American Michael López-Alegría have spent the longest time—215 days—on the ISS. However, the person who has spent the most time in space ever is Sergei Krikaleve. He has flown on six space flights over several years and spent 803 days in space. Altogether, that's more than two years!

Today, that's still what happens. Astronauts lift off aboard Russian spacecraft. Normally it takes about two days to get from Earth to the ISS. But in 2013, a *Soyuz* spacecraft managed to reach the ISS in just six hours!

Once the spacecraft docks with the ISS, astronauts arrive on board and begin their months-long stay on the ISS. There are a lot of things to get used to.

In space, there is no gravity to pull water down, so its surface tension causes it to form spheres.

Today, there is a wide range of meals available to astronauts—but most of it might not look like something you'd eat at home!

Eating

Have you ever eaten space ice cream? It's basically ice cream with all the liquid sucked out.

Space ice cream is a good example of the way that food can look a lot different in space. For example, astronauts can't sprinkle grains of salt on their food in space. The tiny pieces could float away and get stuck in equipment. Instead, they have to use liquid salt.

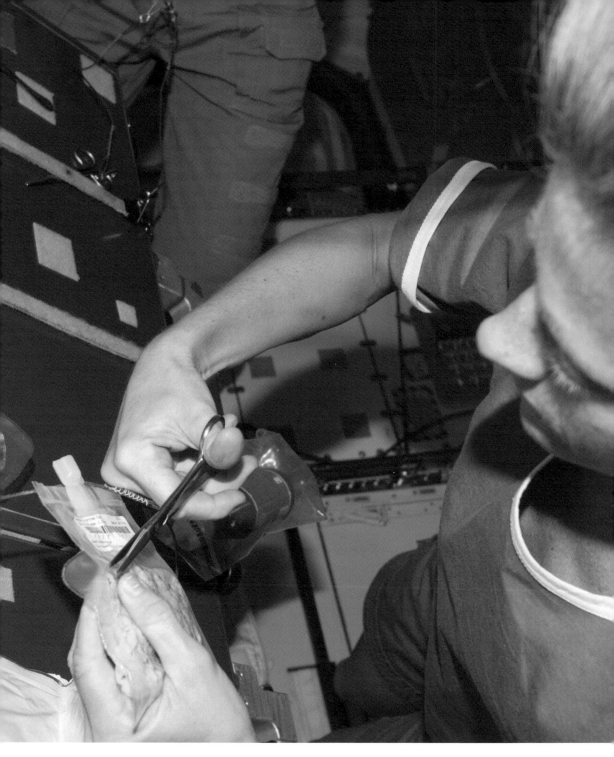

Special packaging helps ensure that food stays fresh for a long time. After all, there's no grocery store in space!

Astronauts eat three times a day, like on Earth. When people first went into space, they had to eat mostly *dehydrated* foods like space ice cream. Today, scientists have come up with tastier choices.

The ISS doesn't really have a kitchen. It doesn't have a refrigerator or a stove or an oven. All the food on board is already cooked. It just has to be reheated or have water added to it.

After living in space for a while, your taste buds start to not work as well. Astronauts can't taste things as well as once they're back on Earth. Foods don't taste the same to them. But astronauts will try to eat spicy or other flavorful foods to get the same kind of experience.

All foods have to be packed in containers when you're living in space. Soups come in bags, for example. Astronauts drink their soup through a straw. Lots of food comes in cans or bags. No one wants food floating away and getting jammed into expensive equipment or stuck to the wall!

When astronauts eat with silverware, they have to be careful their spoons and plates don't float away. They keep them on the table with magnets, bungee cords, and Velcro.

The kitchen table doesn't have chairs around it. Astronauts just float around it while making and eating meals. They also spend some of their free time around the table.

Sleeping

Astronauts' days are *scheduled*, and they have a lot to do. They also have time for sleep, though. Usually they get a full eight hours of sleep each night.

Sleep schedules are important. Up in space, there aren't really days and nights. Astronauts on the space station see the sun rise and set on Earth every forty-five minutes! In other words, they will see the sun rise fifteen times every twenty-four hours. To have a normal Earth schedule, they have to plan their awake times and sleep times.

When something is **dehydrated**, all the water has been removed from it.

Something that is **scheduled** is planned out in advance.

Astronauts must wear space suits to perform repairs on the outside of ISS.

Each astronaut has a very small sleeping cabin. In the cabin is a sleeping bag, where the astronaut can tie him- or herself down for sleep. If astronauts didn't tie themselves down, they would float around in the cabin and bump into things.

Astronauts sleep near *ventilation* fans. If they didn't have a fan nearby, they could end up surrounded by the carbon dioxide they breathe out during the night. The fans push the carbon dioxide away.

Sleeping on the ISS can be hard. The space station is noisy, with all its equipment and fans. Astronauts wear earplugs, or they just get used to the noise.

> ***Ventilation*** is moving air around so it stays fresh.
>
> ***Personal hygiene*** is keeping yourself clean.
>
> Something that is ***edible*** can be eaten.

Hygiene

Just because they're in space doesn't mean astronauts don't have to brush their teeth and wash their hair! It's just a little harder than on Earth.

All the *personal hygiene* stuff that astronauts need is in a kit attached to the wall. If they kept toothpaste and deodorant on a shelf, it would just float away.

The ISS doesn't have washing machines to clean clothes. Instead, astronauts simply wear clothes they can throw away. They wear one set of clothes for three days or so. Then they throw that set away and change into new clothes. Besides, changing clothes is pretty hard in space.

The ISS also doesn't have a shower. A shower wouldn't work very well without gravity. In space, water sticks to people instead of running down them—so instead of taking a shower, astronauts use wet towels to wash. They also use no-rinse shampoo to clean their hair.

When astronauts brush their teeth, they use *edible* toothpaste. They can't just spit it out and rinse it away in a sink. The toothpaste would go everywhere. So they use toothpaste they can swallow.

To use the toilet, astronauts have to strap themselves down. Space toilets don't have any water in them. The toilet sucks away waste into

The tube attached to these hair clippers is a vacuum that sucks away hair clippings. It's important that astronauts don't let anything float around inside the station, because it could get caught in equipment and cause problems.

a tank. Just going to the bathroom can take ten or fifteen minutes longer than it does on Earth. Some astronauts say that using the bathroom is one of the hardest things to get used to on the ISS.

Exercise

Astronauts have to exercise a lot. On Earth, we use our muscles all the time, every time we move around. In space, people don't use their muscles as much because of the lack of gravity. Their muscles lose strength. Their bones also start to get weaker.

To keep their muscles, skeletal systems, and *circulatory systems* healthy and in shape, astronauts have to exercise at least two hours a day. They use special exercise equipment.

Astronauts walk and run on a treadmill. The treadmill actually just floats around the compartment. That way, it can move with the astronaut using it. The treadmill is attached to the astronaut.

Astronauts also use an exercise bike. The bike is attached to the ISS, and the astronauts strap themselves onto the bike.

The third way astronauts exercise is with weights. They have a special piece of equipment that simulates gravity, so it feels like lifting weights. Otherwise, lifting 100 pounds would feel like nothing.

Even with all that exercise, astronauts still often lose bone strength. Scientists are continuing to study how they can help astronauts stay healthy. It's a problem that has to be solved before people can live for longer periods in space.

Working

The reason astronauts are on the ISS to begin with is to do experiments! A big part of an astronaut's day is spent doing *research*.

Astronauts have done a lot different experiments up in space. They have studied flames and how things burn. They have looked at the

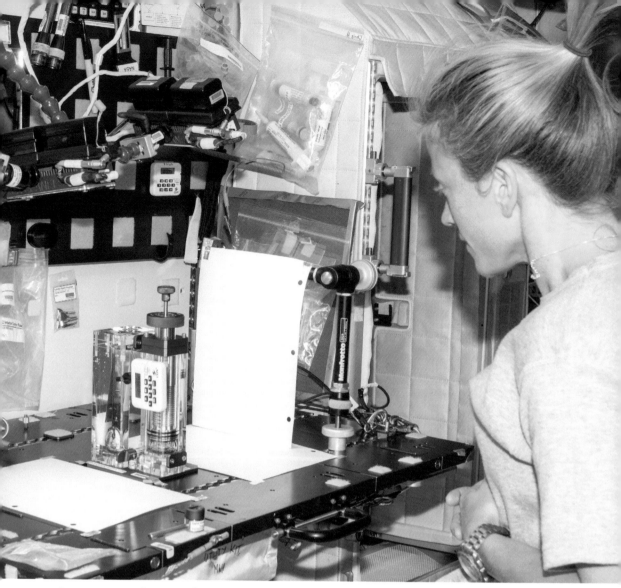

Astronauts often perform experiments on the ISS to see how certain things happen when there is no gravity.

Geology is the study of what the Earth is made of and how it acts.

Something that is **unique** is one of a kind. There is nothing else like it.

geology of the Earth, since they have such a *unique* view of the planet. They have looked into space using the Hubble Space Telescope.

Many of the experiments they do have to do with how the body deals with living in space. They use themselves as labs.

This is the same kind of camera that a photographer on Earth might use—but it needs a space suit of its own to protect it from the vacuum of space.

Some experiments have to do with living in space even longer. If we ever plan on sending people farther into space, they'll have to spend years in space. Some experiments, for example, have to do with growing food in space. Astronauts who travel for years will need to be able to grow and make their own food.

The astronauts also work on keeping the space station in shape. Sometimes things break or need to be replaced. The astronauts on board have to make sure everything on the ISS is working correctly. They fix any problems that are going on.

Even though they live busy lives, astronauts have plenty of opportunities to have fun!

Relaxing

Astronauts don't have to work every minute they're on the ISS. Sometimes they get free time so they can relax.

Some ways of relaxing and having fun are harder in space, like playing cards. The cards just float away if no one is holding onto them.

But astronauts can read, watch movies, talk to their families, use the computer, and talk to one another. They also enjoy looking out the window. Not many people get to look down at the Earth or out into space. Even after a few months in space, astronauts have said they never get tired of looking out the ISS windows.

Find Out Even More

Try typing "International Space Station" into the search bar on Google. com. You'll get millions and millions of results. But the first results will probably include these sites:

International Space Station | NASA
www.nasa.gov/mission_pages/station/main/index.html

International Space Station - Wikipedia, the free encyclopedia
en.wikipedia.org/wiki/International_Space_Station

ISS Tracker
www.isstracker.com

International Space Station | Facebook
www.facebook.com/ISS

And there are millions of other websites to see. Many of them are great places to find more information about the ISS. But not every site in the search results will be a great resource. Some sites are better sources of information than others.

What you search for is a big part of how good your results are. Try searching for "ISS" instead of "International Space Station" and you get very different results.

If you're looking for information on the space station, you

probably don't want to visit the International School Services website (www.iss.edu) or the financial business ISS (www.issgovernance.com). Remember to be as clear in your search as you can be so that you get the best results.

FOUR

What Comes Next?

The very first space stations only lasted a couple of years. As far as space stations go, the ISS is permanent. But "permanent" really only means it will be in space for a decade or two. The International Space Station wasn't meant to last forever.

So what will happen to the ISS in a few years? What will come after it? Scientists are working on those very questions right now.

Retirement

Maintaining the ISS takes a lot of money. And over time, the space station's parts get older and older. They cost a lot to replace or repair. The technology on board also gets older. Newer technology is invented that can

Maintaining something means working on it so it doesn't break or fall apart.

45

The view from inside the ISS as a Russian Soyuz spacecraft departs for home.

ISS: THE INTERNATIONAL SPACE STATION

do more things. Eventually, it just makes sense to build a new space station, instead of fixing an old one.

The ISS will keep going until at least 2020. The countries that run the ISS have promised enough money until then.

However, the ISS might keep going for a little bit longer. Some people think it could still work until 2028 before it has to be *retired*.

Right now, no one is sure just how much longer we'll use the ISS. There are several more *expeditions* scheduled, though. The ISS isn't going to be retired right away.

When it is retired, some parts of the ISS might be *recycled*. We might want to build another space station. Or something else in space. Then we could use some of the parts from the ISS to build something new.

What isn't recycled might be crashed into the ocean. That's what happened to old space stations such as Mir. Crashing the space station will keep it from becoming space junk.

The Future of Space Exploration

The ISS is the biggest project in space right now. Lots of countries are working together to make sure the ISS works right. They are all doing experiments on the ISS and sending astronauts up.

When something is **retired**, it is no longer used.

Expeditions are trips taken for some purpose, like to explore or do science experiments.

When something is **recycled**, it is reused.

Space Junk

Space junk, or space debris, is all that extra manmade stuff floating around in space. People have sent things up into space for only about sixty years, but we've already left a lot of garbage behind. Old satellites, paint flakes, and pieces of rockets are all circling the Earth. Scientists guess there are at least 30,000 pieces of junk bigger than 4 inches out in space, all left behind by humans. All that junk can run into space stations and spacecraft; it could possibly damage them. NASA and the Russian space administration track the bigger pieces of space junk, to make sure they don't crash into the ISS.

To keep the astronauts safe and make sure nothing goes wrong, the ISS is constantly being monitored by mission controllers back on Earth.

The ISS's Cupola provides the best view of Earth. Here, Canadian astronaut David Cassidy takes a picture of a specific point on the Earth's surface.

Eventually, scientists and governments will come up with the next big space project. NASA is looking into the idea of sending people to an asteroid, and lots of people think we'll try to send astronauts to Mars next.

The ISS is like practice for even more space exploration. We need to know how people can survive for a long time in space. The experiments that astronauts have done on the ISS help us figure that out.

We're also learning how to work together to explore space. Getting to Mars, or even beyond, would take a lot of work. One country alone wouldn't be able to do it. We need lots of countries to work together.

The fifteen countries that worked on the ISS have proven that it's

What Comes Next?

Although the ISS will one day be retired, humans will never stop exploring the universe around them!

possible for people all over the world to work together to explore space. Now it will be a lot easier to send people to Mars.

It's hard to say exactly what will come next after the ISS. Space exploration moves very quickly. The first manmade satellite was sent into space in 1957. Just twelve years later, the first person landed on the moon!

Who knows what could happen twelve years from now? By the time you're an adult, we might have landed someone on Mars. Or built a new space station. Or decided on a completely different goal. Space exploration is always changing— and it is always exciting!

Space Tourism

One the most exciting new things in space exploration is space tourism. People can now buy a spot on a spacecraft and go up into space. You don't have to be an astronaut. But you do have to be rich. One ride can cost up to $40 million. Private companies, like SpaceX and Virgin Galactic, bring tourists into space. These companies don't have anything to do with governments, like NASA does. Individual people interested in space exploration own these companies. Spacecraft created by these companies have docked with the ISS, to bring supplies and people. Space hotels might be coming next!

Find Out Even More

Whenever you're searching online, it's important to keep a few things in mind. You should always be thinking about the sites you're visiting and asking yourself a few questions:

1. Who created this website? The website for NASA is a much better source of information on the International Space Station than a personal blog. Remember to think about where the information you're reading online is coming from.

2. Does the information on this site line up with what you can find on other sites? Because anyone is free to create their own website and put up any information they want, not all information on the internet is correct or based on facts. Make sure to look at more than one website to be sure something is true, especially when you're not sure about the source of the information.

3. When was the site made? When was the information you're reading posted? You can often check the date on posts you read on websites. That's important for knowing if the information is up-to-date. If information was posted five years ago, things might have changed. In science and space exploration, things move quickly. Having the latest information is very important. Try to check for dates on websites you're visiting so that you can be sure what you're reading is accurate.

4. Does what you're reading have a certain point of view? Does the writer tell you what she thinks about the subject, or does she just give you the facts? Everyone has a point of view. Young people might look at the world differently from older people. People in Egypt might see the world differently from people in Japan. You might have a point of view that's different from your friends. That doesn't mean you can't be friends, but it's important to keep in mind that people may have different ways of looking at things. This is the same on the internet. Everyone has a way of seeing things that is their own. Knowing their point of view can be a good way to understand their website better.

5. What information can you find on this site that you couldn't find on others? Why do you think that is? Do you think one website left some information out? Do you think that the website's point of view changed what information was included? Which site do you think is more trustworthy? Can you find any other information to back up one site or the other?

6. How is the information on the website given to you? Is it organized in a way that makes the site easy to use or is it difficult to find what you're looking for? What does the site look like? Does that change the way the site works or the way the information is given to you?

7. What do you like about the site? What do you not like? Do you feel like you learned something from what you read?

Here's What We Recommend

If you want to to learn more about the International Space Station and space exploration, here are some good websites and books to get you started!

Online

BrainPop: International Space Station
www.brainpop.com/technology/transportation/internationalspacestation

ESA Kids: Space Stations
www.esa.int/esaKIDSen/SEMZXJWJD1E_LifeinSpace_0.html

NASA Kids' Club
www.nasa.gov/audience/forkids/kidsclub/flash/index.html

Space Station Kids!
iss.jaxa.jp/kids/en

In Books

Catchpole, John E. *The International Space Station: Building for the Future.* Chichester, UK: Praxis Publishing, 2008.

Holden, Henry M. *The Coolest Job in the Universe: Working Aboard the International Space Station.* Berkeley Heights, N.J.: Enslow Publishers, 2012.

Nelson, Maria. *Life on the International Space Station.* New York: Gareth Stevens Publishing, 2013.

Rau, Dana Meachen. *The International Space Station.* North Mankato, Minn.: Compass Point Books, 2005.

Index

About the Author

Kim Etingoff lives in Boston, Massachusetts, spending part of her time working on farms. Kim writes educational books for young people on topics including health, science, history, and more.

Picture Credits